First World War
and Army of Occupation
War Diary
France, Belgium and Germany

41 DIVISION
124 Infantry Brigade
Royal Fusiliers (City of London Regiment)
23rd Battalion
1 March 1919 - 30 September 1919

WO95/2643/6

The Naval & Military Press Ltd
www.nmarchive.com
Published in association with The National Archives

Published by

The Naval & Military Press Ltd

Unit 10 Ridgewood Industrial Park,

Uckfield, East Sussex,

TN22 5QE England

Tel: +44 (0) 1825 749494

www.naval-military-press.com

www.nmarchive.com

This diary has been reprinted in facsimile from the original. Any imperfections are inevitably reproduced and the quality may fall short of modern type and cartographic standards.

© **Crown Copyright**
Images reproduced by permission of The National Archives, London, England, 2015.

Contents

Document type	Place/Title	Date From	Date To
Heading	WO95/2643 (6)		
Heading	London Division (Late 41st Division) 124th Infy Bde 23rd Bn Roy. Fusiliers Mar 1919-1919 Sep From 2 Div 99 Bde. To Rhine Bde		
War Diary	Ehreshoven	01/03/1919	18/03/1919
War Diary	Lindlar	19/03/1919	28/03/1919
War Diary	Kalk	29/03/1919	11/05/1919
War Diary	Overath	12/05/1919	30/06/1919
War Diary	Marialinden	01/07/1919	31/08/1919
War Diary	Volberg.	01/09/1919	02/09/1919
War Diary	Neunkirchen	03/09/1919	22/09/1919
War Diary	Overath.	23/09/1919	30/09/1919

WD 05/SD 05 (6)

WD 05/SD 05 (6)

LONDON DIVISION
(LATE 41ST DIVISION)
124TH INFY BDE

23RD BN ROY. FUSILIERS

MAR 1919 - ~~FEB 1920~~

1919 SEP

FROM LDN 99 BDE

TO 1 RHINE BDE

Army Form C. 2118.

23 R.T.

WAR DIARY
or
INTELLIGENCE SUMMARY.
(Erase heading not required.)

Instructions regarding War Diaries and Intelligence Summaries are contained in F. S. Regs., Part II. and the Staff Manual respectively. Title pages will be prepared in manuscript.

40 T
(2 Bn.)

Place	Date	Hour	Summary of Events and Information	Remarks and references to Appendices
	1919. March			
HINDOVEN	1-10		Training and Recreation daily.	
	11		Inspection of Battalion by Divisional Commander.	
	12-17		Training and Recreation daily.	
	18		Battalion relieves 26th Battalion Royal Fusiliers in the Outpost Line, LINNICH SECTOR. Battn. headquarters at LINNICH. Re-inforcement of 10 officers and 160 Other Ranks arrive from 24th Royal Fusiliers.	
LINNICH.	19-27		Training and Recreation daily.	
	28		Battalion relieved by the 10th Queens. Move to COLOGNE-KALK. 3rd London Infantry Brigade in Divisional reserve. The HAND GRENADE, the distinguishing badge of the Battalion is abolished by higher authority.	
KALK.	29-31			
	April 1-4		The Battalion absorbs the 52nd Bn. Royal Fusiliers. 43 Officers. 760 Other Ranks. Day tours on the Rhine commence.	
KALK.	5-14		Training and Recreation daily.	
	15		Brevet Lieut.Colonel L.A.ASHBURNER, D.S.O., M.V.O., assumes command of the Battalion.	
	16-23		Training and Recreation daily.	
	24		Inspection of the Battalion by Divisional Commander.	
	25-30		Training and Recreation daily.	
KALK.	May 1		Capt. C.A.RUSSELL, M.C., adjutant, vice Capt. H.E.KURN, demobilised.	
	2-5			
	6		Inspection of Battalion by GENERAL SIR WILLIAM ROBERTSON, G.C.B.,K.C.V.O., D.S.O., Commanding-in-Chief, British Army of the Rhine.	
	7-10			
	11		Battalion moves to OVERATH by rail taking over from the 7th Battalion Middlesex Regt. "B" Coy. on detachment at HAU AUEL.	
OVERATH.	12-15		ALBUHERA DAY etc.	

Army Form C. 2118.

WAR DIARY
or
INTELLIGENCE SUMMARY.
(Erase heading not required.)

Instructions regarding War Diaries and Intelligence Summaries are contained in F. S. Regs., Part II and the Staff Manual respectively. Title pages will be prepared in manuscript.

Place	Date	Hour	Summary of Events and Information	Remarks and references to Appendices
OVERATH.	1919 May. 17-26		Training and Recreation daily.	
	27		Battalion War Savings Association formed.	
OVERATH.	June. 1-2		King's Birthday. Ceremonial Parade and a holiday.	
	3		Inspection of Battalion by Lieut.General Sir AYLMER HALDANE, K.C.B., D.S.O., G.O.C., VIth Corps.	
	4		Kalk Football Cup Final, 57th Seige Battery - 2 goals, 23rd Bn.Royal Fusiliers - 1 goal.	
	5-6		Preparations made for the advance into Germany on "J" Day in the event of non-acceptance of Peace Terms.	
	8-19		Instructions for Advance held in abeyance and subsequently cancelled.	
	20		"J" Day.	
	21		Brigade Swimming Gala - Battalion won two-thirds of Prizes.	
	22			
	23-25		"C" & "D" Companies relieve Outpost Companies of 17th Battalion Royal Fusiliers in MARIALINDEN Sector.	
	26			
	28		Signature of Peace.	
	29		Divine Service. Thanksgiving Service for Peace.	
	30			
MARIALINDEN	July 1		Battn.H.Q., "A"&"B"Coys. move to MARIALINDEN Area. Present distribution of Battalion: "C"Coy., Right Outpost Coy., H.Q., gRUTZENBACH. "D"Coy. Left Outpost Coy., H.Q., DRABENDERHOHE. "A"Coy. in support at LANDWEHR. "B"Coy. in reserve at ROHE. Bn.H.Q., MARIALINDEN.	
	3-18		Training & Recreation daily. Cricket, Swimming, etc.	
	19.		Battalion Sports held at KLEF near VILKERATH. Champion Coy. "C" Company.	
	20-21			
	22		Battn. inspected by Major General Sir S.T.B.Lawford, K.C.B., G.O.C., London Division.	
	23		"A"&"B"Coys. relieve "C"&"D"Coys. respectively in the outpost line.	
	24-27			
	28			
	29			

C.N. Turk
Major & Lt.Colonel
Comdg. 23rd Bn. Royal Fusiliers

Army Form C. 2118.

WAR DIARY
or
INTELLIGENCE SUMMARY.
(Erase heading not required.)

Instructions regarding War Diaries and Intelligence Summaries are contained in F. S. Regs., Part II. and the Staff Manual respectively. Title pages will be prepared in manuscript.

Place	Date	Hour	Summary of Events and Information	Remarks and references to Appendices
MARIALINDEN	1919. Aug. 1.		War Savings results for July. Amount subscribed £1137-19-1. Percentage of Members, 51% of Battalion Strength. Battalion top of VIth Corps list for amount subscribed. Pay & Mess Books taken into use.	
	2-10		Training and Recreation daily.	
	8		"D" Company move to COLN-KALK.	
	11		Divisional Inter-Coy Drill and Turn out Competition. 1st "D" Coy. 23rd Bn. Royal Fusiliers.	
	12-15		" "	
	17		Guard of Honour for Army Council found by "D" Coy, 23rd Bn. Royal Fusiliers.	
	18		"D" Company move to VOLBERG.	
	21		Brigade Rifle Meeting.	
	22		" "	
	23-25			
	26		Battalion (less "D" Coy) move to VOLBERG.	
	27-31		Training and Recreation daily.	

E. A. S. Gell
Major.
Comdg. 23rd Battalion Royal Fusiliers.

Army Form C. 2118.

WAR DIARY
or
INTELLIGENCE SUMMARY.
(Erase heading not required.)

23rd R.F.

Instructions regarding War Diaries and Intelligence Summaries are contained in F. S. Regs., Part I. and the Staff Manual respectively. Title pages will be prepared in manuscript.

Place	Date	Hour	Summary of Events and Information	Remarks and references to Appendices
	1919.		**23rd BATTALION ROYAL FUSILIERS.**	
VOLBERG.	Sept 1st		Battalion less "A" Company move to NEUNKIRCHEN Area relieving 52nd Battalion Manchester Regt.	
	2nd		"C" & "D" Companies in Outpost Line. B.H.Q. and "B" Company in NEUNKIRCHEN.	
NEUNKIRCHEN.	3-7		Training and Recreation daily.	
	8		Rhine Army Rifle Meeting at DROVE commences.	
	9		"A" Company rejoins battalion at NEUNKIRCHEN.	
	13		Rhine Army Rifle Meeting ends.	
	22		Battalion relieved by 17th battalion Royal Fusiliers and move back to OVERATH.	
OVERATH.	23-30		Training and Recreation daily.	
			**	
			During the month the battalion has fired the General Musketry Course Part iii, also the Lewis Gun Course.	
			[signature] Capt/Major.	
			Commanding 23rd Battalion Royal Fusiliers.	

www.ingramcontent.com/pod-product-compliance
Lightning Source LLC
Chambersburg PA
CBHW081617160426
43191CB00011B/2165